EXPLORE THE U.S.A.

NORTH DAKOTA

Cindy Rodriguez and Galadriel Watson

LET'S READ
AV²
BY WEIGL™
ADDED VALUE • AUDIO VISUAL

Go to **www.av2books.com**, and enter this book's unique code.

BOOK CODE

AVD26242

AV² by Weigl brings you media enhanced books that support active learning.

AV² provides enriched content that supplements and complements this book. Weigl's AV² books strive to create inspired learning and engage young minds in a total learning experience.

Your AV² Media Enhanced books come alive with...

Audio
Listen to sections of the book read aloud.

Video
Watch informative video clips.

Embedded Weblinks
Gain additional information for research.

Try This!
Complete activities and hands-on experiments.

Key Words
Study vocabulary, and complete a matching word activity.

Quizzes
Test your knowledge.

Slide Show
View images and captions, and prepare a presentation.

... and much, much more!

Published by AV² by Weigl
350 5th Avenue, 59th Floor New York, NY 10118
Website: www.av2books.com

Library of Congress Cataloging-in-Publication Data

Names: Rodriguez, Cindy, author. | Watson, Galadriel Findlay, author.
Title: North Dakota / Cindy Rodriguez and Galadriel Watson.
Other titles: North Dakota (2019)
Description: New York, NY : AV2 by Weigl, 2019. | Series: Explore the U.S.A.
Identifiers: LCCN 2018003685 (print) | LCCN 2018014614 (ebook) | ISBN 9781489674685 (Multi-User eBook) | ISBN 9781489674678 (hard cover : alk. paper) | ISBN 9781489681249 (soft cover : alk. paper)
Subjects: LCSH: North Dakota--Juvenile literature.
Classification: LCC F636.3 (ebook) | LCC F636.3 .R596 2019 (print) | DDC 978.4--dc23
LC record available at https://lccn.loc.gov/2018003685

Printed in the United States of America in Brainerd, Minnesota
1 2 3 4 5 6 7 8 9 0 22 21 20 19 18

062018
102517

Project Coordinator: Heather Kissock
Art Director: Terry Paulhus

Contents

3

I live in the state of North Dakota. It is called the Peace Garden State.

North Dakota has both prairies and very rocky land.

Where Is North Dakota?

North Dakota is in the north part of the United States. Minnesota is to the east and Montana is west. South Dakota is to the south. North Dakota shares a border with Canada to the north.

Bismarck is the capital city of North Dakota. This city is home to the tallest building in the state.

CANADA

USA

Hawai'i

MEXICO

North Dakota

CANADA

NORTH DAKOTA

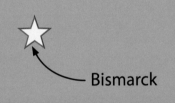

Icelandic
State Park

Red River

MONTANA

MINNESOTA

Little Missouri
National Grasslands

Bismarck

SOUTH DAKOTA

SCALE
0 ⊢ – – – ⊣ 30 Miles

 Capital
City

▲ State
Park

Grasslands

River

7

Climate

North Dakota has short, hot summers. It has long, cold winters. North Dakota gets less rain than most other states.

The coldest part of the state in the winter is the north. The hottest part of the state in the summer is the south.

Beavers are common in the waters of North Dakota. They build their dams during warm weather. Beavers are less active in the winter.

Industry

The largest industry in North Dakota is farming. Many types of grains are grown in the state.

North Dakota grows more wheat than any other U.S. state except Kansas.

The Past

Native Americans were the first people to live in North Dakota. Explorers and fur traders came to the area about 275 years ago.

"In my early days, I was
eager to learn and to do
things, and therefore
I learned quickly."

– *Sitting Bull*

Important North Dakotan

Sitting Bull was a Native American chief. He was known for his great courage. Sitting Bull led battles for his people to keep their land.

Population

More than 750,000 people live in North Dakota today. It has one of the smallest state populations.

Irish and Scottish settlers came from Canada in the 1800s. They grew food for fur trappers and traders.

North Dakota Population Numbers	
1890	190,983
1930	680,845
1970	617,761
2017	755,393

North Dakota Timeline

9,500 BC
Early Native Americans hunt big game such as bison.

1790
Fur traders from Canada visit North Dakota.

1801
Alexander Henry the Younger opens a trading post in Pembina.

Get Online

What is another important event in North Dakota's history?

1803
Lewis and Clark explore North Dakota.

1889
North Dakota becomes a state.

2017
North Dakota has the lowest unemployment rate in the country.

North Dakota Symbols

Nokota Horse
State Animal

Western Meadowlark
State Bird

Wild Prairie Rose
State Flower

North Dakota
State Seal

North Dakota
State Flag

Fun Facts

North Dakota bees produce more than **42 million pounds of honey** a year.

Highway 46 is one of the **longest** stretches of straight **road** in the whole country.

North Dakota grows **more sunflowers** than any other state.

North Dakota produces enough beef to make **2 billion hamburgers** per year.

It is **against the law** to **fall asleep** with **shoes on** in North Dakota.

The **world's largest** **bison statue** is at the Frontier Village in Jamestown. It is **26 feet tall**.

KEY WORDS

Research has shown that as much as 65 percent of all written material published in English is made up of 300 words. These 300 words cannot be taught using pictures or learned by sounding them out. They must be recognized by sight. This book contains 70 common sight words to help young readers improve their reading fluency and comprehension. This book also teaches young readers several important content words, such as proper nouns. These words are paired with pictures to aid in learning and improve understanding.

Page	Sight Words First Appearance
4	I, in, is, it, live, of, state, the
5	and, both, has, land, very
6	a, city, home, part, this, to, where, with
7	miles
8	gets, most, other, than
9	are, their, they, waters
10	any, grown, makes, many, more
13	about, came, first, people, were, years
14	days, do, learn, my, things, was
15	for, great, he, his, important, keep, known
16	food, from, numbers, one
18	as, big, opens, such
19	another, country, what
20	animal
22	at, enough, feet, world's

Page	Content Words First Appearance
4	North Dakota, Peace Garden State
5	prairies
6	Bismarck, building, Canada, capital, Minnesota, Montana, South Dakota, United States
7	Icelandic State Park, Little Missouri National Grasslands, Red River
8	climate, rain, summers, weather, winters
9	beavers, dams
10	farming, grains, industry, Kansas, wheat
13	explorers, fur, Native Americans, past, traders
14	Sitting Bull
15	battles, chief, courage
16	Irish, population, Scottish, settlers, today, trappers
18	Alexander Henry the Younger, bison, Pembina, timeline, trading post
19	Clark, event, history, Lewis, rate, unemployment
20	bird, Nakota horse, symbols, western meadowlark
21	flag, flower, seal, wild prairie rose
22	bees, facts, Highway 46, honey, million, pounds, road, sunflowers
23	beef, Frontier Village, hamburgers, Jamestown, law, shoes, statue

Check out www.av2books.com for activities, videos, audio clips, and more!

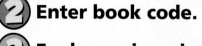

1 Go to www.av2books.com.

2 Enter book code. **A V D 2 6 2 4 2**

3 Fuel your imagination online!

www.av2books.com

24